THE JOURNEY OF AN ANXIOUS MIND

The Tempest in My Head

Meghan Solo

BookLeaf
Publishing

India | USA | UK

Presentation by *BookLeaf* Publishing

Web: www.bookleafpub.com

E-mail: info@bookleafpub.com

ISBN: 9789358361711

First edition 2021

"To my parents, who created a safe
space for a weirdo to express herself
and explore all the strange things that
piqued her interest.

To my sister, who is the light to my dark.

To my partner who stays through the
storm.

To the beautiful friends who keep me
somewhat sane.

To my fur children, and my fur nieces
and nephews.

To those who made my life hell and
made me who I am today.

I thank you.

As above, so below. "

ACKNOWLEDGEMENT

"This would not have happened without immense amounts of therapy, soul-searching, and self-exploration. Sprinkled with dashes of panic and ADHD here and there. I have long wanted to put this collection into a book but would not have been able to do this alone. Everyone who has touched my life in some way has led to this, for better or worse."

PREFACE

"This has not been an easy collection to put together. I typically write my best poetry when I am in my darkest places. I commend you on taking your first step into the journey of an anxious mind. If you can think of something terrible, there is a very solid chance it has happened to me. My joke has long been that I have the back story and history of someone who would make a phenomenal motivational speaker. My only weakness is that I have not accomplished something that society would deem me "worthy" of speaking to others.

I have been bullied. I have been suicidal, to an alarming degree. I have been sexually assaulted. I have a very intense medical condition that means I must plan and alter my life around it to accommodate. I had major surgery in 2020. I am immuno-compromised. I have anxiety. I have depression. I have some pretty gnarly ADHD. There is probably more messed up with me that I cannot think of at this time, but you get the picture.

And yet I am here. I have done it. This is my first book. This is my first moment. And I could not have done this without every single encounter I have had in my life. The good, the bad, the ugly. I would not be who I am today without these experiences. And while it makes for uncomfortable living, it also provides interesting stories and plenty of writing material.

Thank you for buying my book. Even if it is just one of you. Even if it is just my mother (hi mom). If my experiences can offer you insight. Knowledge that you are not alone and I have been there in the depths of hell with you....Then welcome. I love you. Take my hand and we will explore the darkness together and find those places where the light peeks through."

1

"the soul screams

silent

an unwavering pang

aches

wordless wounds

fester

hope falters

eroding

shadows overwhelming

drowning

wandering soul

displaced

trying

fervent desperation

seeking

bound and tangled

lost

a caged bird

cries

the lonely soul

bleeds

shining fears

yearn

inner decay increases

defeat."

2

"I can't breathe.

My chest is a loadstone.

Caving under pressure and expectations.

The crushing weight of dismay.

Riven in two, staring at the paths before me.

One beckons to freedom.

The other to steadiness.

A step one way.

A retreat to the other.

The potent strain ripping through shreds of sanity.

Clinging to the edge.

What if there is a third path?

One where…

I just step off the edge.

Let it all disappear.

In peaceful solace.

Circumventing life screaming in my ears.

Swallow the darkness whole.

A bittersweet farewell.

Please let me leave.

Leave it all behind.

I will flee to the ether.

My absence a gift.

To all."

3

"Displacement and loss.

There is no correct way.

The wheel turns.

Teach them to be free.

The cages only manifest in the dark.

Gilded bars and silver chains.

The muffled gasps.

Pain, pleasure, or somewhere in between?

A slow torture ripping through her veins.

The bound creature cries.

A pitiful sound, straight from the heart.

Pleading for affection.

Begging for kindness.

Craving the cruelty.

Wicked tongues and casual betrayal.

Alert to the slightest hint of light.

Warily licking wounds in the shadows.

Each day creeps closer to the eruption.

A cornered animal knows no fear.

Prepare for claws and teeth and desperation.

A monster unleashed.

This is what you made of me,

She screams into the void.

Before she burns it all down."

4

"The despair creeps in

A slow, sinuous process

Crawling out from my heart

Encapsulating every limb

Until I'm restrained to my very core"

5

"she wanted to be soft

but not in a way that denoted weakness

she wanted to yield with grace

at the things beyond her control

and let the moments reveal

the underlying steel that form

her inner core"

6

"Dishevelled hair,

a gasping breath;

we plead with those

who wish for death.

The helpless gaze,

and broken tears;

A grasping hand

and shuttered fears.

Time inches on

unspoken truths,

as subtle as

excited youths.

Despair alone,

the seagulls cry.

This is not how

we say goodbye..."

7

"drown me in lyrics;

let the words run rampant across the floor.

anything but the inside;

locked behind an iron door.

the poets are restless;

screaming incessantly for more.

bury me in music;

they always say they'll be back for more."

8

"It's not the same,

it's all unknown.

Inside I feel so hollow,

rattled to the bone.

Disillusioned and so scared,

can't find my solid ground.

Everything is frightening me,

jumping at no sound.

The doors are black,

and welded closed.

My breath sticks in my throat,

my inner peace deposed.

It drags me ever downwards,

this weight upon my chest.

Every piece has shattered,

I thought it was my best.

The night are long and aching,

screaming their despair.

A muffled curse inside my room,

I knew that he was there.

The doors are ruined; torn apart,

my castle has been broken.

All that remains, not lost nor found,

my battered form upon the floor,

every hurt unspoken."

9

"Alone.

He's alone.

If he's alone.

Cries if he's alone.

Cries if he's alone here.

Always cries if he's alone here.

Mom always cries if he's alone here.

Mom always cries as if he's alone here.

Mom almost always cries as if he's alone here.

Mom almost always cries softly, as if he's alone here.

Mom almost always cries as if he's alone here.

Mom always cries as if he's alone here.

Mom always cries if he's alone here.

Always cries if he's alone here.

Cries if he's alone here.

If he's alone.

He's alone.

Alone."

"If?

When.

Who?

Wherever.

Stop.

Wrong.

Again.

Believe.

Tried.

How?

No.

Perhaps.

Won't?

Stay.

Try.

Better?

Disbelieving.

Broke.

Retry.

Never.

Always.

Leaving.

Please.

Don't.

Okay.

Go."

11

"If,

 I were of a simpler nature,

Less flighty and wrong,

Would I still be your songbird?

If,

I were sturdy and practical,

A solid rock unmoved, unruffled,

Could I still be your flame?

If,

Sorrow didn't haunt me,

And I was happy all the time,

Would you still be my panic room?

If,

I didn't question everything,

Balk, and fight and not listen to reason,

Would you give up on me?

If,

I wasn't lost,

And still searching for a map,

Would you ask for directions?

If,

I didn't love you,

Would you even still be here?"

12

"Bliss

Distant

Elicit

Distraction

This moment can't end

Carry my heart gently

I fear it may not be whole

Broken and bruised it beats so hard

A little more whole every day

Uncertain and fragile, hope flutters more

Soft sighing smiles, hands brushing gently in sun

Serenity abounds, blissful silence wanders

Patience a never ending pool of healing solace

Cover me in warming affection, wrapped in kind ribbons

Soothing breezes running wild across vast expanses of trust

The mountains barricade my soul, protection from all but you, love

Adventuring traveller, you conquered the frozen heights, unaided

Smashing obstacles, rending barriers asunder, strive ever higher

The pinnacle beckons, unconquered heights daring you to concede, but you don't

Deliver me a promise, a wish, a dream that is granted, encompassed in your soul."

13

"The moon emerged,

slipping through the clouds.

Weary bones aching in the chill.

A slow meander across the barren wasteland.

Soul aching loneliness,

Soft, steady weeping.

Disavows our secret thoughts. "

14

"Cheeky grin,

Hard eyes,

Dark as sin,

Fresh lies.

Wrong choices,

Hushed cries,

Stifled voices,

Breathless sighs.

Stolen moments,

Touching thighs,

Wasted innocence,

Prince's guise.

Her fairy tale,

Initial highs,

Tip the scales,

Naïveté dies.

A floating dream,

Belatedly wise,

His usual scheme,

The stolen prize."

15

"An unending road,

windows down.

The music lingers,

like the touch of your hand on mine,

Your smile teases,

Stealing me away from the dark places
my mind

calls home.

I cannot linger there.

A serenade of love and loss.

Heart brimming full,

As life

Moves on.

Sucker punched by the unexpected,

 Forever moving forwards,

Slogging on.

You are my happy place,

The unforgotten song.

Wind tears through my hair,

It's always a disaster

Whenever you are near.

But it cannot be stolen,

This breathless, tumbling sensation,

Pouring through my mind.

My soul craves your presence.

Can we go for another drive?

Just you.

     And me.

The music.

     Two hearts.

The road.

     Just drive. "

16

"I cannot stop.

The flutter,

an inexplicable tingle.

Total inability to explain.

I wish you could feel my soul

singing as you touch me.

I pray you get to experience the same sensations I get,

spending all of my days with you.

If I could bottle my joy and gift it to you,

I would give it all and more.

I am the queen of dark faces,

mistrusted places,

broken spaces.

You never give up on me.

A stubborn immovability to keep on succeeding.

I can never say thanks in the depths of
how I truly wish."

17

"the sky was perfect.

the last lingering traces of sun to my
right,

hints of golden pink,

slowly deepening into the richest shades
of blue and black i have ever seen.

a light breeze stirred my hair,

bringing the smell of the water to me,

while the trickling of the pond quivered
in the background.

the odd sound of a car passing by my
only hints of civilization.

my porch swing was moving slightly,

pressing against my spine,

rocking gently,

the north star my only companion.

alone; except for a celestial body billions
of miles away.

and i realized,

the only thing missing....

was you."

18

"The days are long

the nights even longer

These are the ones that ever hunger

Crying out their fierce war song

I stand alone under a tree

anxiety clouds my every thought

My brain screams for all of it to stop

Never does a single sound escape from
me

He is before me

Offering a hand

This shall be the grounds of my last
stand

He will help me to fly free

One step forward

That's all I say

What I can get done today

But the win feels weak and blurred

I take two back

Where I remember

That happy, loving, pre-December

I now begin to see my lack

I will prevail

I want to shout

But ever crippled with self-doubt

It's no surprise this too shall fail

I cannot change who I have been

The record stands unchanging

The armies are arranging

Victory goes to my demon or my inner
Queen

The demon it has always grown

Feeding on my fears and faults

Forcing my strengths inside a vault

Whispering so damnably, "you will
always be alone..."

It cackles and advances

A rare gleam lights it's eyes

The Queen transfixed and trembling
utters out a cry

"We must stand strong for love will be
our chance!"

His proffered hand on days of turmoil

The reality I cling to

Can I be strong enough to finally break
through?

I feel like I'm a toil

Ever falling short of expectations

He cannot wait forever

But can he hold his faith in hoping I am clever

Battling and seeking out my needed revelations

As I hold him in high regard

Can he run with me unwavering

Trusting me and my mind with our crippled labouring?

Or have his views been marred?

The breath is ripped our of my lungs

An anvil crushes my chest

The nights refuse to give me rest

My journey a tale unsung."

"The clouds crawl by.

Trickling through the sky like wandering children.

Your voice surrounds me.

Friendly.

Anecdotal.

Pleasant.

A lingering sound, wrapping me in comfort.

Breeze stirring my hair as you dash about madly.

I am stillness in the chaos.

Rock in a hurricane.

I become shelter.

Protection.

Refuge.

Yours."

"Tangled

Unpolished

Breathless

Unrelenting

Irrepressible

Dilation

Whisper

Entrancing

Integration

Elevation

Relief

Exquisite

Tantalizing

Sensation

Feeling

Palpitation

Hesitation

Intoxication

Happenstance

Presentation

Falsification

Separation

Testimonial

Elucidate

Repressed

Exacerbated

Wrecked

Dilated

Illuminated

Unrepentant

Backdated

Underrated

Tormented"